True Love

Mark Anthony

For my one and only Bird, the light and true love of my life.

A heartfelt thank you to all of my readers from around the world who follow me on social media, liking, following, commenting, and sharing my work. I could not do this without you.

Other works by Mark Anthony

The Beautiful Truth

The Beautiful Life

Love Notes

PART 1

Confession

Whenever
I open
a book,
I am always
looking
for the story
of us.

The Reason Why

I keep writing you these poems
to remind you how much I love you,
when days are long,
and life pulls us
in opposite directions
like twin tides,
one pulled by the sun
the other by the moon.

I keep writing you these poems
because words are the only way
I know how to touch your heart
when we're days, hours,
or seconds apart.

Mystery

Some dreams we don't have names for,
some eyes speak to us without words,
and fill us with light and color.

Some loves enter our lives,
as invisible as oxygen,
yet sustain us for a lifetime,
which is why I believe
in the endless miracle of you.

Invisible Kingdoms

I'm in bed with her,
laughing at nothing.

Such treasures,
kings only wish for,
as they send out
armies of the blind,
searching for Kingdoms
they'll never find.

*It's Never too Late to Have a Happy
Childhood.*

It amazes me
how long
you can hold on
to hurt;

How just a small
dagger of ice
can poison
a single word
that lingers
for ages
inside your heart,
and then
one day
you hear
another word,
so softly spoken
it melts
the ice
into tears,
and you are back
where you
started from,
only bolder,
wiser, and
a little more
innocent.

Learning to be Alone.

Learning to feel,
learning how to be
somebody
without her
was something
I never thought
I could do,
but in time,
there were days
when she didn't even cross
my mind,
and it wasn't her
I was sad for
anymore.

It was that life
had moved on,
and I was no longer
the same person
with a broken heart.

I was somebody ready
to fall in love
with you.

Before We Met

I could almost see you
standing in the sunlight,
with your perfect smile,
your laughter,
and unending grace;

And I wondered,
how long does love live
as a dream,
before it becomes
a prayer?

How many poems
would I have to write,
before they become you?

Advice to Young Men

Look inside and ask what the feeling is.

Don't be afraid to feel,
be speechless, sad,
lonely or confused.

Have the courage to grieve
your frozen feelings,
because time is a river
that waits for no man,
and tears
are the only way
to let go of the shore.

Don't keep pouring whiskey
on your wounds
or you will grow
a garden of regrets.

Learn to love the simple things,
like old trees, and cleaning your room.

Discover what it means to be
the secret genius of silence,
with a deep knowing smile.

Truth

You have to go through
a few fakes,
before you find
a real one.

Hope

I hope that one day
you find the love you deserve.

I hope one day
you find the love
that inspires your best self.

I hope one day
you find the love
that gives you peace,
and makes you believe
that dreams come true.

Blessing in Disguise

One day
you will discover
that your pain
was just pointing
to the places
where you
most needed
to heal.

Patience

You won't meet
the right one
at the wrong time,
my dear,
because timing
in love
is everything

Definition

Don't be fooled
by the word "love,"
as it means
many different things
to many different people,
but your task, my dear,
is to find out
what it means
to him.

TRUE LOVE

Forgiveness

All that I knew of love
was what not to do,
how not to drink
and be numb,
how not to run away
from myself.

And so I arrived
on your doorstep,
like a blank page,
an open book,
a love story,
waiting to be written
with you,
in the stars.

Letting go

"How do you know
when it's over?"

"When you can look at them
without anger or remorse,
and know they
were not the one."

The Wrong One

Sometimes his eyes said, "forever,"
and sometimes
they said, "not today,"
and each day
she would look into his eyes
like a child peeling petals
from a flower
to see if he loved her
      or loved her not.

Look Inside

Sometimes
we mistake
what we want
to cultivate
in ourselves,
in the form
of another--

No wonder
he wasn't enough;

he was only part
of who
you wanted
become.

Snake Charmers

My mother once told me:

Be careful of those
with too much charm.

They might not know
how to turn it off.

Rare

You deserve somebody
who knows why you're rare.

Stuart's

The first time we talked
it was cold outside,
and we acted as if it was over
before it began,
and nothing vulnerable
could be said
without freezing,
and so I said,
we should go inside
to where it is warm.

Inside the cafe,
it was warm,
and you were
such a wonderful
contradiction
of torn blue jeans
and roses,
I felt as if I had
finally found
my dark angel.

The Truth

The truth breaks curses,
and so whatever curse
had been keeping you
from me
was broken the moment
I told you that you were beautiful,
because I was looking
at more than just your body,
I was looking at your soul.

One Thing at a Time

I didn't kiss you
the night we met,
and didn't want to.

I knew that kisses
would come in time,
and a kiss is nothing
compared to a love
that's true.

Imagination

And then it snowed
for three days,
and three nights,
and we couldn't go anywhere,
but each other's arms,
and we told each other stories
about the future,
and where we imagined
we might be
in ten years,
and though I never told you,
in every story,
all I really knew
was that I saw myself there
with you.

Win-Win

Once I had learned to be happy with myself,
I would wait for nobody but her,
because nobody else could add
to the peace I already had.

Souls

I don't understand
how people can't see
the soul behind the eyes,
the spirit that lives
and breathes inside
every human being,
when that is all I look for,
and why I fell in love
with you.

Look

Just look closely
around you,
and you will see
all the little treasures
of the world
scattered like yellow leaves,
children playing in the grass,
old men sitting on a park bench,
young people writing poetry
in their schoolbooks.

You don't need money
to be rich;

You just need eyes
to see the poetry
that belongs to
everyone,
if you know
where to look.

Something in the Way

She has a way about her
that is as alluring
and radiant
as the summer sun;

and sometimes
when I look at her
I have to squint my eyes
just to see her smiling
through the bright
and falling air.

The Wait

I promise you
the wait will be worth it
in the end,
because you've always
been designed
for something
bigger and better.

There Are Some People

Who don't want to be led into sunlight,
some people whose lives are so small, bitter and dark,
they'd prefer to stay under the rocks and stones of
their cave,
than to venture outside,
where love might rain over them
at any moment.

So don't waste your time judging them;

They've already judged themselves as guilty,
condemned themselves to solitary confinement,
while serving a life sentence
for crimes you may never know.

Jack Pot

There was a time
I didn't know you,
When the world seemed so empty,
I would wonder what I was doing on this earth,
Other than waiting;

But when you came into my life,
the world suddenly filled with new colors,
sounds, and fragrances,
that made me feel truly alive.

You brought with you
all the gifts of the universe,
and made me lucky in love.

Wait for Them

I waited for you
the way frost waits for sunlight
to kiss it into Spring;

I waited for you
the way the moon waits for poets
to sing its praise,
and an onion waits
for tears of innocence.

I waited for you
because I had no choice;

It was either you,
or nobody
or nothing at all.

Day and Night

I love to hold her in the quiet
just before dawn, as the blueness of night
is erased by the sun,
and I love to let her go,
and wait for her to return.
so that I can dream of her,
the way I did before we met,
when she was still a fragment of sunlight
missing from my soul,
a name whispered on the wind
that would one day find my lips,

Until You

Until I met you,
I only knew
different ways
to say, "Goodbye."

Never Forget Your Strength

You've driven lions from their den
with just the wound of your voice,
and forged lightning
with the tip of your tongue.

Never forget all the foes you have vanquished
along the way,

The ghosts,
The demons,
The dragons.

And you are walking forward still,
like a hero with your own name.

Never forget.

The Journey

She feels it in her heart,
and in her soul,
and down to her very bones.

The universe is colliding
within her.

She is on a journey
to find herself.

And she is already home.

Fuck the World

The world will lie to you,
and tell you to put your faith
into money, television, and pills.
The world will lie to you
and tell you not to care,
and that nothing matters.

But the poet inside will tell you,
the world has always been
full of shit,
and so love it anyway.

Carry on,
and enjoy all the mad
and infinite contradictions,
of what it means to be alive.

Simplicity

The years pass without a sound,
and your hand stays in mine,
as we walk this earth
like careless children
admiring the rivers and the shadows,
eating fresh fruit,
and laughing with the wind.

There is no paradise greater
than the one I hold in my hand,
as the years pass,
and the flowers
come and go like summers
rising into a sky of blue.

Spots of Time

I was reborn the moment
I touched your face,
and felt the tenderness
of seeing with sincere
and open eyes.

I felt as if I had known you
all my life, as if you'd always
been beside me but
I'd been to blind to see.

Enjoy the Silence

Sometimes
we need no words,
no sounds
to break the silence.

All it takes
are soft touches,
and the electricity
of the soul
to connect us
to a new place
where all
is communicated,
and nothing
is left
unsaid.

The Word is Not the Thing

Love is so many things
there are times
when I don't know
why we give it a name;

It would be just as easy
to point to the night sky,
burning with mad
and lonely stars
and let the silence
speak for itself.

Existential

Sometimes
the universe
is so breathtakingly beautiful,
and terrifying,
I can only describe it
with tears of silence

She

She is strong and soft,
loyal and beautiful.

She knows her worth,
and is courageous
to the end.

She has no regrets
because she's
learned her lessons,
and truly loves herself.

It's OK to Feel it.

Sometimes
we forget
that happiness
is not the only
beautiful thing
in the universe,
and that sadness
can cleanse us
in a way
that feels
just as divine.

Sooner or Later

I know it's not easy,
doing what you know
in your heart
you have to do,
but the sooner you let go
of what's killing you,
the sooner you do,
the sooner
you
will find the love
that will heal you,
even if that love
is for yourself.

Proof

"How do you know,
she's the one?"

"I've always been
a better man
with her,
than I was
without her."

Confusion

As a young man,
I confused love with power,
and thought a woman would only love me
If I owned the world.

But as I got older,
I saw how power grows weak with time,
and that trust is far more rare.

And only love
is strong enough
to make people stay.

Oxygen

Sometimes we take love for granted,
and forget
how it is like the oxygen
we need to survive.

And it is only when we lose it
that we discover
we can't breathe.

PART 2

Lonely

Maybe we feel lonely
when we're afraid
to let others
see us
for who we really are,
so we push them away
with who we aren't.

Peace

What a beautiful thing it is
to wake up next to somebody
who was always meant to be there.

Together and Apart

Sometimes
I will sit alone
on a park bench
and watch the birds,
and think
how true love is
like two birds sharing
the same sky,
but also enjoying
their own flight.

Paradise

There is a secret paradise
that exists
inside of all of us,
and when
somebody
touches it,
it stays with us
forever.

Tale of Two Cities

Everyone lives between two cities,
one built by hands of power,
and the other built
by hands of love
and each moment
we decide which one
we want to live in,
and how much
we want to sacrifice
in order to live there.

Time Travel

If you could do it over, go back in time,
and change events,
what would you do differently?

What decision would you retreat from,
as you walked backward in slow motion
without the wisdom you gained from
going forward, and the knowledge
you earned from your mistakes?

Who would you be without the tears that
rebuilt you into who you are now,
and if you don't like who you are now,
what can you do now,
to change yourself for the future,
so that you would never want
to go back to the past?

No Scripts

To have a real relationship
you need to know what it feels like to be present,
open, alive, and vulnerable;

Otherwise, you are only protecting yourself
with habits, and not seeing the person
for who they are,
only for who you need them to be
for your own comfort.

Keep on Keeping on.

Keep growing.
Keep changing.
Keep Evolving.

You were never
meant to be,
anything less
than loved.

Into the Wild

We learn things
only to forget them.

We become impatient
with our lives
when the terrain
doesn't match the map
we've been given.

So tear up the map,
and really look around you.

See how everything,
including the moon and stars,
is exactly where it's supposed to be.

How Do I Know if it's True Love?

The right one will make
all of your questions disappear,
and you will feel like you're always
in the right place at the right time.

Deprogramming

Over the years I've learned
it is more important to listen than to speak,
to open up, rather than close,
to be vulnerable rather than safe,
and that nearly everything I had been taught
about being a man was wrong.

Grace

There is nothing like
the moonlit horizon of your body,
the curves that rise and fall
like your breathing in the quiet dark.

And I am thankful for this moment,
this moonlight,
and for the earth,
for bringing you to me.

Think About It

Letting go of somebody
who is wrong for you,
is also stepping toward
somebody who is right.

Attitude of Gratitude

Each day is a new day,
full of possibility and hope,
and each day she chooses
to see the light and love
that surrounds her,
and even when times are hard,
she's still grateful for everything
life has given her.

She's Changed

You can see it in her face,
and in her walk,
and in the way
she knows where she's going,
and doesn't look back

No Time for Maybes

You better believe she's the one,
with all your heart and soul,
because life will try to break you apart,
and make you surrender,
and anything less than true love
will snap like a brittle branch,
so you better know
with all your heart and soul,
she's the one,
and always will be.

Be Prepared

Be open
to the infinite
possibilities
of the universe,
because you never know
when true love
will find you.

Fragile Things

She told me life
was a bouquet of flowers
and we needed to pick something beautiful
each day to remember,
so that we learn
to appreciate the beauty
of fragile things.

And in time
I realized
even her words
were like soft petals
falling from her mouth,
and into the naked river
of my soul.

Your Eyes

Your eyes sustain me
through long days and night.

Your eyes of gratitude,
Your eyes of sadness,
Your eyes of sunlight,
Your eyes of sand,
Your eyes of fresh fruit,
Your eyes of fire.

Your eyes that hold
everything I love,
and nourish me
to my bones.

Love Story

It's so easy to forget
that sometimes love
is just listening
without judgement
or agenda,
but with an open heart
and mind,
and a willingness to see
your story in mine.

Longing

Sometimes my longing for her
is like a boy's longing for the moonlight
to peek into his bedroom,
and bathe everything in silver light,
just to remind him
the world is woven together
with hidden magic
too beautiful to explain.

Perfect Pictures

We want true love to be a perfect picture
full of perfect smiles,
and sunlit plazas,
but the more I learn about love,
the more ordinary the pictures I see,
sometimes out of focus,
sometimes awkward
or in the wrong light.

Because true love still takes pictures
on dark and cloudy days,
when you can't see the sunset,
but you know in your heart,
it's still there.

Body of Woman

Moonlit hills full of dreams
and distant trees, opening up
to the moon and stars,
smooth skin spilling secrets
into a flight of birds,
whispering over me
as I lie still.

I have no choice
but to surrender
to your infinite calm,
your change of seasons,
your fire, your rain,
your touches
that bless me
like something sacred
and fill me
with
the wonder
of falling stars.

Inspiration

Live life.

Don't be afraid to say "yes" to your dreams.

Leave town.

Find something you are passionate about, and lose
yourself in it.

Discover the hidden mysteries of your heart.

Explore the depths of your being.

Trust in change.

Never doubt the ground you walk on
is anything less than a miracle.

Advice for Men

Don't fall for a woman
who is anything less than your best,
one who challenges you
while others would let you sleep.

Look for the one who makes you strong,
not weak, and one who can see
the true depth of your soul.

Find the one whose beauty radiates
even when she sleeps,
and whose laughter rings like church bells,
and when you find her,
never let her go,
for she is your very soul.

The Hero's Journey

I was a sailor lost at sea,
listening for the sound of your singing
upon the waves,
looking for a reason to let go of the wheel.

And I finally woke up,
half drowned
along the rocks,
but I never blamed you
for the shipwreck,
because I knew
it was the storm
I needed
to bring me
to you.

Time Tells Us if it's True

When you tell somebody you love them,
the word doesn't mean much
beyond a sweet sound,
until time passes,
and you know what it's like to hold them
when the world is falling apart,
and everything is stripped away
but the naked soul,
without pride or vanity.

Then and only then,
will you know
what love means,
and only if you don't look away,
look deeper, and hold them closer.

Through the Storms

Feelings can come and go
like the tide,
but our love remains
as constant as the ocean,
and deeper
than the storms
that break into sunlight,
and leave the water
glistening like strings of fresh pearls.

Anchor

She wants to feel
the love beneath your words,
and see the truth in your smile,
and when nothing
in the world make sense,
she wants you
to put all the broken pieces
back together,
and show her
how they all
lead back to love.

Still True

If only I could tell you
once and for all,
how you opened me to another world
where the sky is always blue
and the sunlight played upon the water
like music.

And your laughter
was like the echo of everything I held dear,
then I would never have to write
another poem,
because everything I've said before
is still as true today, my love,
as it was,
on the day we first met.

Never Take Her for Granted.

Look at the way she lights up the room.

Listen to how her voice reminds you
everything will be okay,
and even though you see her every day,
remember she's a gift from the sea,
and don't forget
the infinite joy
she brings.

Bloom

Lift yourself up
to the sky,
and let your smile
tell everyone
you don't care
anymore
what other's say.

You are simply
one badass flower,
doing what
you do best
and
that is,
to bloom.

My Love

My love for you
is wild and fierce,
and down to the bones.

My love for you
is chaos,
and magic,
and moonlight,
and everything
beautiful
than can't be
defined.

Let Me Love You

Let me love you
With a humble heart,
And an open mind.

Let me listen
To the music
Of your voice,
As if it was
The very song
Of the earth.

Let my love for you
Open you
Like a flower
To the sun
Until
I am completely
Yours.

Habits

We all get weak
and fall
into old habits;

So wake up,
and see them,
break them.

Do something different
and when you feel
your strength
coming back to you,
know that it's your soul
thanking your body
for listening.

Time

There comes a time,
when only a soulmate will do.

Desire

Let me undress you
the way fire undresses the dark,
the way the sun undresses
winter,
kiss by kiss
devouring
the cold,
and leaving
only fresh flowers
and Spring rain,
and you
breathless
in the wind.

By Any Other Name

You can go your whole life,
not believing in fate or destiny,
and then one day,
you find somebody
so right for you,
at such the right time and place,
you won't know what else to call it.

A Poem About Love

Love is a walk in the rain,
a leaf blowing across the street;

Love is a glance,
a whisper, a song,
an insomnia.

Love is a waiting line,
a bouquet of questions,
a promise to be somebody new,
and to always stay the same.

Love is a confusion,
and a certainty,
a waking up to discover
that after all
the sparks,
the flames,
and the smoke,
somebody is still there.

Nothing Compares

Whatever the world says about love
is nothing compared to what it is,
and so, my love, I ask you
to fill in the spaces between words
with everything you know
in your heart to be true,
and know this is still not enough
to tell the story of how I love you.

Thank you for giving me your days,
and your smiles, your laughter
and your tears;

Thank you for your faith
and your doubt, and all the colors
in between;

Your love has filled my life
with treasures
and is the reason why
I believe true love
isn't just found in fairy tales.

Dark Night of the Soul

Even in my darkest days,
I knew I was on a path,
that somehow my suffering
was meant to be,
but it was only when Grace
tapped me on the shoulder
and whispered,
"You don't have to kill yourself
for the love of others,"
that I truly began to love myself.

The Speed of Light

I can't save you
from your past
or hold you
when I wasn't there,
but I can listen to you
when you tell me
what it was like to be so alone,
and hold you now,
in my arms
so closely
it will collapse
all time and space,
and give you love
at the speed of light.

Nobody Loves You
the Way I Love You,
My Love.

I'm not afraid
to swim the depths of you,
to see your honor,
your grace,
your stubbornness,
your raw beauty,
your blue moods,
and quiet rages,
to touch your solitude,
and share your joy.

Nobody loves you
the way I love you,
my love,
because nobody
sees you more
deeply
than me.

Every Little Thing

I'm trying to type away
the blue notes of twilight
as the traffic creaks,
and the muffled voices of strangers
cast off into the night.

She's singing in the shower,
and each note is like a flower tossed to sea.

I want to write, but I can't concentrate
on anything, but the sound of her voice,
and the bare anticipation she brings
with the water shutting off,
the clack of the shower door,
her wet footsteps slipping across the floor,
as she presses her wet body against by back,
and kisses me on the neck
like a feathered angel drenched with rain, erasing
everything I wanted to write
With the poetry of her body,
the soft touch of her lips,
dripping like music
into my thirsty unwritten soul.

All or Nothing

I will never love
just one part of her,
but every broken piece,
every lost and lonely fragment.

My love will gather it all,
and give it back to her.

My love will cherish
the searching,
and the finding,
the pain and the joy,
because that is what love does,
and it is what keeps us together
like the sun and moon.

Perfect Imperfections

We think we have to be perfect
to show our faces to the world,
not knowing there is no such thing.

We're all works in progress,
so it's better go forth
with an open heart,
stumbling here and there
on your quest for love.

In time we will meet
where we all meet,
and wonder what took so long
to see everything
has always been perfect
as it is,
and love
would not have it
any other way.

Body and Soul

It isn't only the body
that pulls me toward you
like the moon to the sea,
but the way you move,
the soft ballet of wind and tide,
the flowers hidden beneath each step,
and your voice,
how it sings to me like a song,
reminding me of apple trees,
honey,
and smoke.

it isn't only the body
that pulls me toward you,
but everything
you are,
from spirit to bone,
flesh to fantasy,
breath, note,
and fire.

Picture Us

Sometimes I feel
like there is only one thing
I want to capture in words,
and it is a picture of you and me
and we're walking along
the river in Paris,
and there is the only
the lonely sound
of boats
heading off to other seas,
and my hand
is in your hand,
and everything else
disappears.

Peace 2

Love,
is not a war
between
the sexes
but a discovery
you are on
the same side.

True Love

I once heard somebody once say
that love doesn't last
and after the first blush of a romance fades,
it disappears like sunlight
at the end of the day.

But I say that true love is what doesn't fade,
and stays standing in the dark,
when everybody else
has walked away.

Patience

There came a time in my life
when no other woman would do, but you,
and even though we'd never met,
I knew you were out there,
waiting for me,
the way I was waiting for you
and so I waited
and didn't fall for the others
no matter how brightly they smiled
or charmingly they spoke.

I knew they weren't you
because they lacked the spark
that ignites the flame,
the sugar that sweetens the coffee,
the heart that can't hide from the world
because it's far too big.

Happily Ever After

Every old couple
holding hands in the park,
is a fairy tale
come true.

True Story

I found myself speechless
when we first met,
because she was as beautiful
as a woman in a novel,
and as sultry as the sunlight
sparkling on the sea;
and so,
when she asked me,
"Are you just going
to pass me by?"

I stammered, said, "No,
of course not,"
and I meant it so much,

I made her my wife.

P.S.

There,
in the silence
between words and actions,
between sight and desire,
wind and tide,
I will hold you,
forever in my life,
forever in my dreams,
forever in my heart.

To Be Continued…

About the Author

Mark Anthony is a bestselling poet
from Seattle whose previous works include,
"Love Notes," "The Beautiful Life," and "The
Beautiful Truth."

He is happily married to his one true love, and
continues to live the life he's always wanted by being
bold, and following his heart.

You can follow him on Instagram
@markanthonypoet

Made in the USA
Columbia, SC
12 December 2019